KATHARINE HEPBURN

A Hollywood Portrait

KATHARINE HEPBURN

A Hollywood Portrait

Sarah Parker Danielson

This edition published in 1993
by SMITHMARK Publishers Inc.,
16 East 32nd Street,
New York, New York 10016.

SMITHMARK books are available for bulk purchase for sales promotion and premium use. For details write or telephone the Manager of Special Sales, SMITHMARK Publishers Inc., 16 East 32nd Street, New York, NY 10016. (212) 532-6600.

Produced by Brompton Books Corp.,
15 Sherwood Place,
Greenwich, CT 06830.

ISBN 0-8317-4283-6

Printed in Hong Kong

10 9 8 7 6 5 4 3 2 1

All photos courtesy American Graphic Systems except:
Brompton Picture Library 83 (bottom), 96, 97, 107 (all)

Designed by Ruth DeJauregui

Page 1: 'Acting is the most minor of gifts,' Hepburn once said. 'After all, Shirley Temple could do it when she was four.'

Previous page: Cigarette in hand, Hepburn strikes a sultry pose for this publicity shot from the 1930s.

Facing page: The pride of Bryn Mawr. Some have likened Hepburn's accent to the sound of a buzz saw. One unknown sage declared her 'a cross between Donald Duck and a Stradivarius.'

INTRODUCTION

Both on screen and off, Katharine Hepburn is famous for her independent nature and indomitable spirit. Though various biographies differ on the date of her birth, Hepburn, in her typical forthright manner, declares in *Me*, her autobiography, that she was born on 12 May 1907 in Hartford — 'despite everything I may have said to the contrary.' Her family was regarded as rather unconventional. Her father, Thomas Hepburn, was a respected surgeon, but he specialized in urology — not an area that was comfortably discussed — and he was a crusader against venereal diseases. He was also an exceptional athlete and encouraged all his children to be athletic.

Hepburn's mother, Katharine Martha Houghton, grew up in a socially prominent family — the Houghtons had founded Corning Glass Works — which made her liberal beliefs all the harder for her traditional neighbors to comprehend. Like her husband, she was an ardent crusader. A strong advocate for women's rights, she was among the early suffragettes who picketed Woodrow Wilson's White House. Guests at the Hepburn household included fellow activists Emma Goldman, Charlotte Perkins Gilman and Emmeline Pankhurst, a British suffragist.

Like her mother, Hepburn attended Bryn Mawr, where her grades were poor until she realized she had to do well in order to be allowed to act in college plays. Her most memorable college role was Pandora in *Woman in the Moone*, an Elizabethan pastoral. Though she majored in history, drama was her true calling, and upon graduation she left for Baltimore to join the Edwin H Knopf Stock Company. She was cast in a small role in *The Czarina*, receiving favorable enough reviews to land a part in Knopf's next production, *The Cradle Snatchers*. This time nerves got the better part of Hepburn, causing her to have difficulties with her voice. Kenneth McKenna (later the head of the MGM Story Department) suggested she study voice under Frances Robinson-Duff, one of the leading voice coaches of the day. Hepburn heeded his advice and went to New York to work with Miss Robinson-Duff. Meanwhile, Knopf had moved his

Facing page: Katharine Hepburn became a star almost immediately after she arrived in Hollywood, but her screen career soon suffered a series of setbacks, just as her stage career did. Hepburn, however, was always able to overcome any obstacle.

company to New York for a production of *The Big Pond*. Hepburn was offered the part of understudy and did such a wonderful reading that she replaced the leading lady. This was too good to be true—only a month in the theater and she was already a star! On opening night, however, she lost her composure during the performance and was summarily fired.

Fortunately for Hepburn, Arthur Hopkins, a Broadway producer, was in the audience and offered her a part in *These Days*, but it closed after only eight days. Next, Hepburn was assigned to understudy Hope Williams in *Holiday*, but she abruptly left the cast to marry Ludlow Ogden Smith on 12 December 1928. After playing the role of housewife for two weeks, Hepburn convinced her new

Above: Audiences were disturbed to see Hepburn dressed as a man in **Sylvia Scarlett** (1935).

husband to move back to New York, where she went back to Hopkins to see if she could reclaim her understudy role. To her surprise, he was expecting her. She filled in for Miss Williams for only one performance, but a few years later, the leading role would be Kate's—this time on film with Cary Grant.

Hepburn was beginning to establish a name for herself on Broadway. It seemed she could get any role she wanted, but she also seemed to have an uncanny ability to get fired. However, with her trademark resiliency, she always landed another plum part. After playing Antiope in *The Warrior's Husband*, she attracted the attention of Hollywood's top

Above: With her classically chiselled cheekbones, Katharine Hepburn was one of Hollywood's most beautiful stars...and one of its most outspoken.

producers and signed a contract with RKO for $1500 a week. (Her salary on Broadway was $150 a week.)

She arrived in California wearing an odd-looking hat and a designer dress that was totally inappropriate for the ninety degree Pasadena heat. To make matters worse, her eye was swollen shut from steel shavings that had become embedded in her eye during the train ride. Myron Selznick of RKO could only shake his head in disbelief. Despite this inauspicious beginning, Hepburn proved herself with her first film, **A Bill of Divorcement** (1932). She truly became an overnight star and won her first Oscar for **Morning Glory** (1933), only her third film. Hepburn, however, did not conform to the typical star image. She hated the press, refused to give autographs, and wore trousers and no make-up. Above all, she always made her opinions known — and Kate had an opinion on everything.

Hepburn received critical acclaim for **Little Women** (1933), but her rise to fame began to decline with her next film, **Spitfire** (1934), which received mixed reviews. A return to Broadway in *The Lake* was greeted with disdain, and her performance prompted Dorothy Parker to remark that Hepburn's 'emotions ran the gamut from A to B.'

Hepburn's films in the 1930s were a mixed lot. Although she starred in such delightful films as Howard Hawk's **Bringing Up Baby** (1938), she was labeled box office poison by the decade's close. Not to be beaten, Hepburn returned to Broadway, where she triumphed in *The Philadelphia Story*. The film version paved the way for her Hollywood comeback.

After **The Philadelphia Story** (1940) she starred in **Woman of the Year** (1942) and so began a lasting relationship, on screen and off, with her costar, Spencer Tracy. Legend has it that upon meeting Spencer Tracy for the first time, Katharine Hepburn remarked, 'I fear I may be a little too tall for you Mr Tracy.' To which he retorted, 'Don't worry — I'll cut you down to size.' While there may be more myth than fact to this witty exchange, it's the sort of banter that characterized their on-screen relationship. Having recovered from the era of box office poison, Hepburn had established herself as a witty, independent heroine, but her career needed a new direction: She found it with Spencer Tracy. Though still possessing an indomitable spirit, Tracy softened Hepburn's rough edges.

The pair made nine films together: **Woman of the Year** (1942), **Keeper of the Flame** (1942), **Without Love** (1945), **The Sea of Grass** (1947), **State of the Union** (1948), **Adam's Rib** (1949), **Pat and Mike** (1952), **The Desk Set** (1957) and **Guess Who's Coming to Dinner** (1967).

The best films that Hepburn made during the 1940s were the films she did with Spencer Tracy, and she began to be thought of as one half of a team. In the 1950s and early 1960s, however, she was recognized as a superior actress in

Facing page: Hepburn's popularity has endured for 60 years, but she is modest about her success, saying: 'I was fortunate to be born with a set of characteristics that were in the public vogue.'

her own right. Beginning with **The African Queen** in 1951, Hepburn starred in a number of roles that proved her mettle as an actress: **Summertime** (1955), **The Rainmaker** (1956), **Suddenly, Last Summer** (1959), and **Long Day's Journey into Night** (1962). When Spencer Tracy's health faltered, she stayed away from the screen for five years, returning for their final film together, **Guess Who's Coming to Dinner** (1967), for which she won her second Academy Award. After Tracy's death, she immediately returned to work and gave a tour de force performance as Eleanor of Aquitaine in **The Lion in Winter** (1968) for back-to-back Oscars.

Though approaching her seventies, Hepburn remained active in film, on television and on stage. In 1981, she appeared with another screen legend, Henry Fonda, in **On Golden Pond** and won an unprecedented fourth Academy Award. An avid gardener and painter, in recent years Hepburn has embarked on a new career as a writer, publishing a book on the making of **The African Queen** and her autobiography, Me. Still as forthright as ever, Hepburn likens herself to an old monument that we will all miss when she is gone. Indeed we will, Kate.

Above: This portrait of Katharine Hepburn captures her luminescent beauty.

Facing page: Whatever her age and whatever the role, Kate always had a sparkle in her eyes.

KATHARINE HEPBURN

Above: Hepburn's first film, **A Bill of Divorcement** (1932), was directed by George Cukor, who had picked Hepburn on the basis of her screen test. Years later Kate would view the screen test and laugh, wondering what Cukor had ever seen in her. Soon after filming of **A Bill of Divorcement** began, he knew his instincts had served him right. 'Kate had absolutely no film experience,' he later remarked, 'but she seemed immediately at home in front of the camera. [John] Barrymore was playing her shell-shocked father — a virtual stranger to her since she was a child. She looked at him with the most enormous tenderness and her eyes filled with tears. After that scene, Jack and I gave each other a look of OK. We knew that we had latched on to something very special.'

Facing page: An early publicity still, taken in 1932 soon after Hepburn arrived in Hollywood.

A Bill of Divorcement (1932) starred Billie Burke (*above*) and John Barrymore (*below*) as a World War I shell-shock victim (Barrymore) who escapes from an asylum and returns home just as his wife (Burke) is about to marry another man. Hepburn (*facing page*) played the daughter who abandons her plans for marriage to devote her life to her ailing father.

These pages: Though she could not avoid glamour shots like these, Hepburn was not the typical Hollywood star. She wanted no part of the Hollywood scene with its parties and premieres, hated the press and avoided her fans. Her behavior earned her the name Katharine of Arrogance.

Above: Hepburn's third film was **Morning Glory** (1933). She discovered the script while waiting to meet with producer Pandro Berman. Noticing a script on his desk, she began reading it and told Berman she must do the film. He told her the part was intended for Constance Bennett, but Hepburn insisted, 'ME, ME, ME!' He gave her the part and she won the first of her four Academy Awards for her performance as Eva Lovelace in **Morning Glory** (1933), the story of a struggling young actress in New York City who perseveres despite a series of setbacks.

The story was so close to Hepburn's own that she added a great deal of depth to the character, rising above a rather limited script. Audiences flocked to see the film and it was clear that Hepburn was the attraction.

Above: A scene from **Morning Glory**. Her costars were Adolphe Menjou and Douglas Fairbanks, Jr, who was quite smitten with her. For weeks, Fairbanks had been trying to get Hepburn to go out on a date with him. She finally consented, only to end the evening early with a headache. He took her home and was so thrilled to actually have spent some time with her that he stayed outside her house, just thinking about her. Suddenly, Kate ran out of the house and drove off with another man.

Above: Hepburn once said, 'I strike people as peculiar in some way, although I don't quite understand why; of course, I have an angular face, an angular body, and I suppose an angular personality which jabs into people.'

Facing page: The play of light across those famous cheekbones bring out Hepburn's classic beauty in this sublime portrait from Hollywood's Golden Age.

Above: The stars of **Little Women** (1933): Joan Bennett as Amy, Jean Parker as Beth, Katharine Hepburn as Jo and Frances Dee as Meg.

Hepburn was delighted to be working with George Cukor again for her fourth film, **Little Women**. Based on Louisa May Alcott's novel about the four March sisters as they grow up while their father is away in the Civil War, Cukor's **Little Women** remained remarkably true to the novel, and is considered the finest screen version of Alcott's book.

Little Women won an Academy Award for Best Screenplay Adaptation (Sarah Y Mason and Victor Heerman) and was nominated for Best Picture and Best Director. Hepburn won the Cannes International Film Festival award for Best Actress.

Facing page: The March sisters. With four films completed in a year, Hepburn was ready to return to Broadway to do *The Lake*. RKO wanted her to do one more film but promised to conclude filming by the time rehearsals for *The Lake* began. The film, **Spitfire** (1934), was unlike anything she had ever done before. It concerned a faith healer in the Ozark Mountains who kidnaps a dying baby and is nearly lynched by her neighbors. A poor, uneducated mountain girl (with a Southern accent) was so far removed from the real Katharine Hepburn that audiences had a hard time accepting Kate as Trigger Hicks.

Above: Hepburn as Jo, the independent idealist of **Little Women** (1933). In director George Cukor's words, '[Kate] was born to play Jo. She's tender and funny, fiercely loyal, and plays the fool when she feels like it. There's a purity about her. Kate and Jo are the same girl: I could go with whatever she did on the set.'

Facing page: In an era when women were expected to wear dresses, Hepburn shocked Hollywood by wearing slacks. Her trademark attire became symbolic of her independent and rebellious nature.

Above: With the the completion of **Little Women** (1933), Hepburn had done four films in the space of a year and was ready to return to Broadway to do *The Lake* (1933). Ultimately, she may have regretted her decision, for *The Lake* was a total disaster.

Facing page: Hepburn as Lady Babbie in **The Little Minister** (1934). Based on the play by JM Barrie, the film concerns an aristocratic woman (Hepburn) who disguises her herself as one of the local gypsies to help them improve their lot in life. She falls in love with the town's minister (John Beal), but the townspeople disapprove of the romance until her true identity is revealed. **The Little Minister** had been filmed twice before (both times as silents) and on stage had been a favorite role of the legendary stage actress Maude Adams. RKO spared no expense for its version and proudly proclaimed 'only the greatest actress of her time could have breathed life into the most magnetic heroine of all time.'

husband to move back to New York, where she went back to Hopkins to see if she could reclaim her understudy role. To her surprise, he was expecting her. She filled in for Miss Williams for only one performance, but a few years later, the leading role would be Kate's—this time on film with Cary Grant.

Hepburn was beginning to establish a name for herself on Broadway. It seemed she could get any role she wanted, but she also seemed to have an uncanny ability to get fired. However, with her trademark resiliency, she always landed another plum part. After playing Antiope in *The Warrior's Husband*, she attracted the attention of Hollywood's top

Above: With her classically chiselled cheekbones, Katharine Hepburn was one of Hollywood's most beautiful stars...and one of its most outspoken.

These pages: Scenes from **The Little Minister** (1934).
Though the story had been well received in the past, its time
had come and gone and the film lost close to ten thousand
dollars, giving Hepburn two failures in a row. RKO was in a
quandary over what to do with her. Its solution was **Break of
Hearts** (1935) with Charles Boyer. Like **The Little Minister**
before it, **Break of Hearts** was a complete failure.

Overleaf: Lady Babbie in her gypsy disguise with Gavin
Dishart (John Beal) — the little minister.

Hepburn's career was faltering. Her last three pictures had flopped and RKO was worried. Her contract called for four more films and the studio would lose a considerable amount of money unless it could find a suitable film for Hepburn. Pandro Berman, head of RKO, finally decided to cast her in the title role in **Alice Adams** (1935) (*above*), based on Booth Tarkington's 1922 novel about a young woman who tries to rise above her social class.

Hepburn's contract gave her choice of director, and had George Cukor been available she would have selected him. RKO suggested William Wyler or George Stevens, both relatively inexperienced. She choose Stevens, who was best known for his two-reel comedies. On the set, however, Hepburn had moments when she must have regretted her decision. On one memorable occasion, director and actress had a heated argument over a scene in which Alice runs up to her room and cries. Hepburn wanted to throw herself on the bed and cry into a pillow because that is what she would have done. Stevens insisted that while Hepburn might keep her tears to herself, Alice would sit at the window and cry. Moreover, he wanted to juxtapose her tears with the rain outside the window. He won — through a window wet with rain, the audience sees a melancholy Alice, tears rolling down her face. Stevens received praise for his faultless direction and went onto great success, reaching the height of his career in the 1950s.

Above: The script for **Sylvia Scarlett** (1936) was by British writer John Collier, who was known for his sophisticated and daring work. Cukor was concerned that Collier's script might be too daring and added a prologue and finale with Hepburn in 'normal,' woman's dress.

Above and below: On the set of **Sylvia Scarlett**. The man on the left is director George Cukor. Cukor was one of Hepburn's closest friends and the two of them worked on a total of 10 films together. Hepburn was a great admirer of Cukor, but during this particular film she recorded in her diary 'This picture makes no sense at all and I wonder whether George Cukor is aware of the fact, because I certainly don't know what the hell I'm doing.'

Facing page: An intriguing still for **Sylvia Scarlett** (1936).

Overleaf: Hepburn's performance in **Sylvia Scarlett** (1936) was well received, but the film as a whole was a disaster. Now, however, it has quite a cult following among Cukor, Hepburn and Cary Grant fans.

These pages: These 1935 portraits provide a unique and dramatic interpretation of Hepburn.

These pages: Hepburn in the mid-1930s. Throughout her career, Hepburn had the ability to inspire, as well as infuriate, her directors. Frank Capra, her director in **State of the Union** (1948) once said, 'There are women and there are women—and then there is Kate. There are actresses and actresses—then there is Hepburn. A rare professional-amateur, acting is her hobby, her living, her love. She is wedded to her vocation as a nun is to hers, and as competitive in acting as Sonya Henie was in skating. No clock-watching, no humbug, no sham temperament. If Katharine Hepburn made up her mind to become a runner, she'd be the first woman to break the four-minute mile.'

After **Sylvia Scarlett** (1936), Hepburn wanted to play Viola in *Twelfth Night* under the direction of Max Reinhardt. However, RKO wouldn't let her out of her contract, and Hepburn would have to wait until 1950 to do Shakespeare, when she played Rosalind (*above*) in *As You Like It*. 'The part of Rosalind,' Hepburn explained, 'is really one of the great tests of how good an actress you are, and I want to find out.' To help ensure her success, Kate insisted that Michael Benthall of the Old Vic direct the production, and she trained for three months with Constance Collier, a veteran of classical theater. Kate's performance was highly regarded, and the show had a successful run of 145 performances.

Facing page: Hepburn's early athletic training gave her marvelous poise and agility. Howard Hawks said of her, 'She has the most amazing body — like a boxer. It's hard for her to make a wrong turn. She's always in perfect balance. She has that beautiful coordination that allows you to stop and make a turn and never fall off balance. This gives her an amazing sense of timing. I've never seen a girl that had that odd rhythm and control.'

These pages: Katharine Hepburn as Mary, Queen of Scots. After the failure of **Sylvia Scarlett** (1936), producer Pandro Berman declared that he would never work with Hepburn again. Even so, she was his choice for **Mary of Scotland** (1936). Maxwell Anderson's play, with Helen Hayes in the title role, had been the hit of the 1934-1935 theater season, but it failed to translate well to the screen.

Mary Stuart should have been an ideal role for Hepburn, but the dominant personalities of both the character and the actress were suppressed. John Ford, Hollywood's number one director at the time, concentrated on the pageantry of the era rather than on the personal drama of the character, which made for a visually exciting but otherwise dull film.

Still, most critics gave Hepburn favorable reviews and she was able to sign a new contract with RKO, guaranteeing her $200,000 for four films.

Above: Katharine Hepburn by Clarence Sinclair Bull, one of Hollywood's finest portrait photographers. As the head of MGM's portrait gallery during Hollywood's Golden Age, Bull helped make MGM synonymous with glamour. He was as important to an emerging actress as was the publicity department. The stars whose images he helped craft include Greta Garbo, Joan Crawford and Norma Shearer.

Facing page: Though her dress has an air of masculinity, Hepburn evokes complete femininity.

Above: Hepburn with Lucille Ball and Ginger Rogers in **Stage Door** (1937). Initially, RKO had planned to give top billing to Ginger Rogers, who was then one of Hollywood's most popular stars, but audiences at the previews responded so positively to Hepburn's performance that RKO gave her top billing.

Based on the Edna Ferber-George S Kaufman play, **Stage Door** is about Terry Randall (Hepburn), a wealthy young woman who desires to become an actress. She lives at The Footlights Club with a group of aspiring actresses, but Terry's wealth and arrogance set her apart from the others. To help her succeed, her father has financed a play, giving her a part that belonged to one of her roommates at The Footlights Club. Depressed at the loss of the part, the young woman leaps to her death from a window.

The plot bore some resemblance to **Morning Glory** (1933), the film that had garnered Hepburn an Oscar four years earlier, and RKO was betting that the similarities would work to its favor. They did — **Stage Door** was a huge hit. Though the plot may sound clichéd, the script was witty and bright.

Director Gregory La Cava encouraged his actors to improvise, but Kate (*facing page*) preferred to thoroughly rehearse a scene, and so when her character's big moment on stage occurs, Hepburn used a well-rehearsed line from *The Lake*: 'The calla lilies are in bloom again,' which became part and parcel of all Katharine Hepburn imitations.

Above: Hepburn's costars for **Bringing Up Baby** (1938) were Cary Grant and Baby, a leopard. Grant played the part of a stuffy anthropologist, while Hepburn played Susan Vane, an heiress determined to marry him. Baby helped to provide the comic element. Hepburn enjoyed working with both her costars: Grant was 'wonderful and funny,' the leopard, 'excellent.' To make sure that the scenes with Baby went smoothly Hepburn wore perfume to make the leopard playful and resin on her shoes to prevent a fall that would upset the leopard. The leopard's trainer said, 'I think if Miss Hepburn should ever decide to leave the screen she could make a very good animal trainer. She has control of her nerves and, best of all, no fear of animals.'

This was Hepburn's first comedy, and her initial tendency was to laugh at everything she did. Director Howard Hawks explained that what made comedy work was that the characters were extremely earnest about everything they did. Hepburn altered her approach, making Susan a delightfully funny character. As was typical of Hepburn, she had her moments when she clashed with Hawks, but in general each had a high regard for the other.

Above: Though today **Bringing Up Baby** (1938) is considered a classic, it was released just when the public began to tire of screwball comedies. The film did not do well at the box office, and contributed to Hepburn's reputation as box office poison. About the time the film came out, the Independent Theater Owners published a list of stars they considered box office poison. Headed by Hepburn, the list included such illustrious names as Marlene Dietrich, Greta Garbo and Joan Crawford. RKO took the list seriously, and in an effort to get rid of Hepburn, offered her a part in a low budget movie, **Mother Carey's Chickens**, with the stipulation that she star in the film or buy out her contract. For $220,000, Hepburn ended her relationship with RKO, sure of her ability to find the right role at the right salary.

These pages: Hepburn's next film paired her again with Cary Grant in **Holiday** (1938) in the role that she understudied on Broadway early in her career. Cary Grant played the part of the free-spirited Johnny Case who wants to see the world on holiday before he settles down and works. Engaged to marry a wealthy young socialite, he instead finds a kindred spirit in her sister (Hepburn) and falls in love with her. Donald Ogden Stewart wrote the script based on Philip Barry's play. Stewart, incidentally, had appeared in the Broadway production as Nick Potter.

Hepburn was in her element. She was working with her favorite director, George Cukor, and a costar she respected in a story that suited her perfectly. The end result was a sparkling comedy satirizing the idle rich. **Holiday** received rave reviews and Hepburn was superb, but she couldn't shake the box office poison label.

Holiday was produced by Columbia Studios, then just a fledgling name in the movie business.

These pages: Hepburn in the late 1930s, during the 'box office poison' era. While under this shadow, Kate found herself fighting for a once in a lifetime role—Scarlett O'Hara in Margaret Mitchell's **Gone With the Wind** (1939). Kate believed she was perfect for the part. David O Selznick, who was producing the film, didn't agree. Though he at first told her he would consider her, he never took her seriously, feeling it was a bad business decision to go with someone who was unpopular with the public. Hepburn confronted him, demanding to know why he didn't want her for a role that was made for her. He finally told her he just couldn't see Clark Gable chasing her for 10 years. She stalked out of his office declaring, 'I may not appeal to you, David, but there are men with different tastes!'

These pages: Katharine Hepburn in **The Philadelphia Story** (1940), the film that resurrected her career. The role was perfect for her, which isn't surprising since she helped Philip Barry with the script for the Broadway play.

Above: A famous scene from **The Philadelphia Story** (1940). Cary Grant's role as the flippant ex-husband was tailor made for him, Hepburn's Tracy Lord was even better than her highly acclaimed stage role, and Stewart's performance earned him an Academy Award for Best Actor. The film also received nominations for Best Picture, Best Actress, Best Supporting Actress, Best Director and won the award for Best Screenplay, written by Donald Ogden Stewart. Hepburn, and most of the general public, felt that she had been snubbed by the Hollywood community since the Oscar went to Ginger Rogers for **Kitty Foyle**. Hepburn, however, did win the New York Film Critics Award.

Facing page: The wedding dress that Hepburn wore for **The Philadelphia Story** (1940) was almost an exact copy of the dress she had worn as a bridesmaid in her own sister's wedding.

Above: Katharine Hepburn and Spencer Tracy in **Keeper of the Flame** (1942), a suspenseful love story based on IAR Wylie's novel. Audiences liked the Tracy-Hepburn pair, but director George Cukor was disappointed with the film because he felt it lacked the tension needed in a thriller.

Facing page: When Spencer Tracy was suggested as a possible leading man for **Woman of the Year** (1942), Kate's response was 'Oh—I don't know. I wonder whether we would be good together. We're so different.' Tracy had a similar reaction when the idea was posed to him. They may have had misgivings, but audiences were delighted with the combination. A new Hepburn persona had emerged—still strong-willed she had found her match in Spencer Tracy. Hepburn earned her fourth Academy Award nomination for the role of Tess Harding.

Overleaf: Tracy and Hepburn complemented each other perfectly. The critic for the *Baltimore Sun* wrote, '[Tracy's] quiet, masculine stubbornness and prosaic outlook on life is in striking contrast with her sparkle and brilliance. They make a fine team.' For movie goers across America they became the 'perfect American couple' for the next quarter of a century.

These pages: **Without Love** (1945), the third Tracy-Hepburn, film, fared better on the screen than it had on stage, thanks to the witty script by Donald Ogden Stewart and the addition of Spencer Tracy to the cast. With its reworked script and strong supporting cast, **Without Love** became the perfect light-hearted Tracy-Hepburn film, which was just what audiences of 1945 needed.

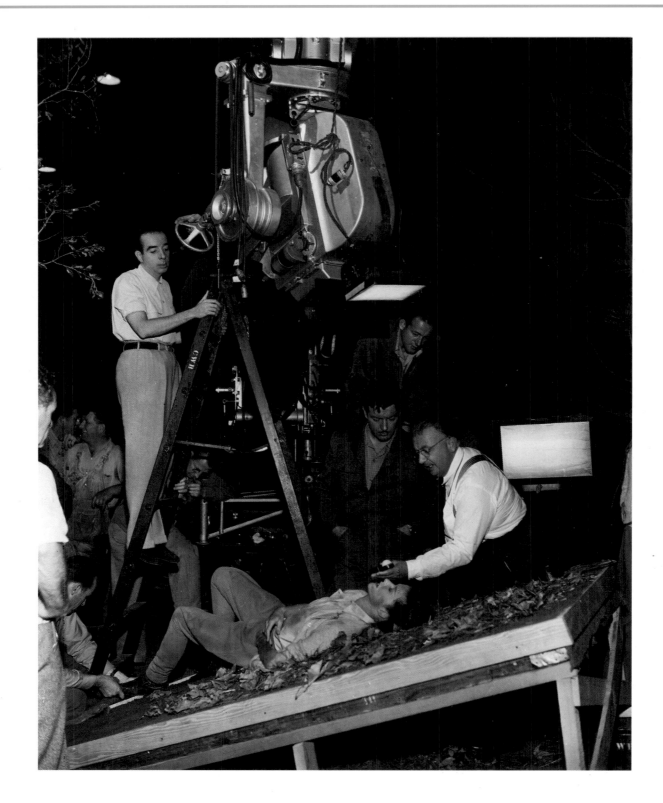

Above: A behind the scenes look at **Undercurrent** (1946), a thriller with Robert Mitchum and Robert Taylor, seen here standing over Hepburn. The man seated near her is Karl Freund, co-inventer of the light meter, using the instrument he invented 11 years earlier. On the ladder is director Vincente Minelli, who was well known for his musicals. Both he and Hepburn were novices at suspense, and the film suffered for it.

Facing page: The plot of **Undercurrent** (1946) concerns a woman who marries a wealthy industrialist (Taylor). He tells her that he has a psychopathic brother, but when she meets the brother (Robert Mitchum) she begins to suspect that it is her husband who is the psychopath.

Right: Pandro Berman, who had produced some of Kate's favorite films at RKO, before moving to MGM, had persuaded her to do **Undercurrent** (1946). They both probably regretted it, with Berman undoubtedly recalling his promise to never work with her again. **Undercurrent** reinforced the idea that Hepburn was at her best as half of Tracy and Hepburn. On her own, MGM just didn't know what to do with her.

Overleaf: A pivotal scene from **Undercurrent** (1946). The male leads were two of Hollywood's top stars. For several years, Robert Taylor had been one of MGM's leading romantic stars, second in popularity to Clark Gable, and Mitchum, who had only recently gained recognition, was earning quite a following for his rugged nonchalance.

The films that Hepburn made without Tracy during the 1940s were some the worst of her career, and some critics have suggested that her career would have faltered completely after **The Philadelphia Story** (1940) had MGM not stumbled onto the winning Tracy-Hepburn combination. However, that's not to say that everything they did together was a smashing success.

Sea of Grass (1947) (*these pages*) stands as a notable exception. This Elia Kazan Western left both its leading stars looking completely out of place. Kazan, a director who favored the method school of acting, was put off by Tracy's straightforward approach, and even more dismayed that the studio insisted the movie be filmed on a set rather than on location. Though the movie was about the grasslands of New Mexico, Kazan bemoaned the fact that nary a blade of grass was in sight.

Based on Russel Crouse and Howard Lindsay's Pulitzer prize-winning play, **State of the Union** (1948) (*these pages*) provides a biting look at the American political process. Kate played the estranged wife of a presidential candidate (Spencer Tracy) who pretends to be happily married to help him win the nomination. When she realizes that ambition has destroyed his principles, she persuades him to withdraw from the race. The film also starred Angela Lansbury (*above, far right*) in one of her first major roles as the domineering Kay Thorndyke, for which she was nominated for an Academy Award. The scenes with Katharine Hepburn and Angela Lansbury are some of the film's best.

    State of the Union was directed by Frank Capra. Many critics consider it Capra's best work because it is stripped of the sentimentality that characterizes **Mr Smith Goes to Washington** (1939) and **Mr Deeds Goes to Town** (1936).

These pages: **State of the Union** (1948) made MGM realize that the talents of Tracy and Hepburn were best suited to comedy rather than a period piece like **Sea of Grass** (1947), so the studio was careful to select just the right film for America's favorite couple: **Adam's Rib** (1949). A comedy about married lawyers who end up on opposite sides of the courtroom, **Adam's Rib** was written by another famous couple, Garson Kanin and Ruth Gordon, and directed by George Cukor. The Kanins were close personal friends of Tracy and Hepburn and it was said that they modeled the roles of Adam and Amanda Banner after the pair.

Kanin and Gordon were nominated for an Oscar for their engaging screenplay. **Adam's Rib** also launched the film career of Judy Holliday, who had just scored a big hit with Garson Kanin's play *Born Yesterday*. She played the defendant accused of shooting her philandering husband.

Above: While on tour in *As You Like It*, Hepburn was contacted by producer Sam Spiegel about a film he was doing with John Huston based on CS Forester's novel *The African Queen*. After reading the novel, Hepburn recognized a great part in Rosie and was anxious to do the picture. She met with Spiegel and the two discussed all the possible leading men, considering only English actors because the character was supposed to have a cockney accent. Then Spiegel suggested Humphrey Bogart and they both knew that he was perfect.

Though Huston had been eager to have Hepburn play Rosie, shortly after arriving on location in Africa he began to fear that she was all wrong for the part, for she was playing the scenes with a too solemn expression. In a flash of brilliance, Huston told her to play Rosie like Eleanor Roosevelt visiting wounded soldiers in the hospital — with a smile on her face. Though the situation may be grim, Rosie should appear to be an optimist, always looking onward. Hepburn considered that the 'best piece of direction' she had ever heard.

Filming was marred by insects, heat and wildlife and finally had to be completed in London after Hepburn and a good many of the crew became ill with dysentery. Huston and Bogey, who had vowed to drink only Jack Daniels until they returned to the States, remained healthy.

Above and below: Scenes from **The African Queen** (1951). Bogart won his only Oscar for his portrayal of the hard-drinking skipper. Hepburn's Rosie earned her a fifth Oscar nomination, and though she lost the Oscar to Vivien Leigh (who years ago had beaten her out of the role of Scarlett O'Hara in **Gone With the Wind** [1939]), Hepburn showed all her detractors that she was ready to move beyond battle-of-the-sexes comedies. It marked the beginning of a new stage in her career, as a true actress, capable of playing roles ranging from a 51-year-old spinster to a powerful queen. **The African Queen** also earned Oscar nominations for Best Director and Best Screenplay.

Above: After **The African Queen** (1951), Hepburn went back to Hollywood to work with the same team that had had such great success with **Adam's Rib** (1949): director George Cukor and screenwriters Garson Kanin and Ruth Gordon, and, of course, Spencer Tracy. Looking a good deal younger than she had in **The African Queen**, Kate put her athletic abilities to work in **Pat and Mike** (1952) as Pat Pemberton, a college physical education teacher who turns professional athlete. Spencer Tracy played her promoter.

Above: The Kanin-Gordon script was filled with the lively banter that audiences had come to expect from a Tracy-Hepburn film, including such memorable lines as 'She ain't got much meat on her, but what she's got is choice.' Kanin and Gordon earned another Oscar nomination for **Pat and Mike**. This was the last film Hepburn made under her MGM contract, and it also marked the last time Tracy and Hepburn worked with George Cukor on a Garson Kanin-Ruth Gordon script.

Above: In 1954, Kate eagerly agreed to work with David Lean in **Summertime** (1955), based loosely on Arthur Laurents' play *The Time of the Cuckoo*. A decade earlier Lean had achieved fame with **Brief Encounters** (1945), and at this point in her career was noted for his intimate dramas. (In later years, his trademark would be grandiose epics.) **Summertime** is the story of Jane Hudson, a spinster who fulfills a lifelong dream of vacationing in Venice. While there she falls in love with a married man and has a brief affair. The bittersweet ending finds her sorrowful, though richer for the experience. Hepburn was nominated for an Academy Award for her performance, and Lean won the New York Film Critics Award for directing. In Britain, the film was released as **Summer Madness.**

Above: Hepburn with Rossano Brazzi, her Italian lover in **Summertime** (1955). While on location in Venice, Hepburn insisted, as she always did, on doing her own stunts. In one famous scene she had to fall backward into the Venice canal. (Today, the spot where she fell is a highlight on the tourist route.) Unfortunately for Kate, the heavily polluted waters of the canal caused an eye infection which plagues her with weeping eyes to this day.

Right: After **Summertime** (1955) Hepburn played another spinster, Lizzie Curry, in **The Rainmaker** (1956). The action takes place in a small southwestern town that is plagued by a drought. A con man named Starbuck (Burt Lancaster) convinces the townspeople that he can bring rain to their parched fields, wooing Lizzie in the process.

The film was based on the Broadway play by N Richard Nash, and was directed by Joseph Anthony, who also directed the stage version. The supporting cast included Lloyd Bridges, Wendell Corey, Earl Holliman and Cameron Prud'Homme, recreating his stage role as Lizzie's father. Both Lancaster and Hepburn were praised for their performances, with the critic for *The London Observer* declaring 'Burt Lancaster has never played the mountebank more sweetly, and Miss Hepburn's performance as the plain, unwanted woman who finds that it is within her own power to become both beautiful and desired, again compels admiration for her qualities as an actress and the choice architecture of her face.'

Summertime did well at the box office, earning Hepburn her seventh nomination for an Academy Award. An Academy Award nomination also went to Alex North for the musical score.

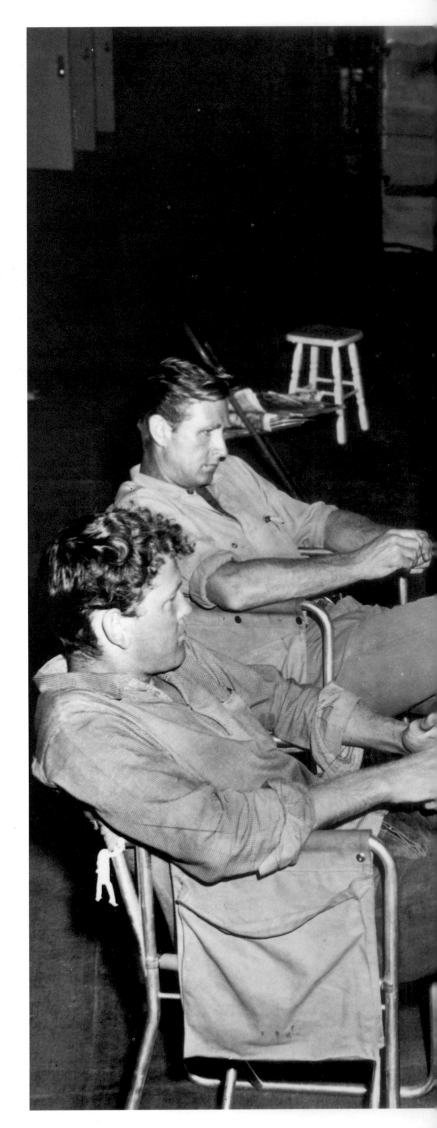

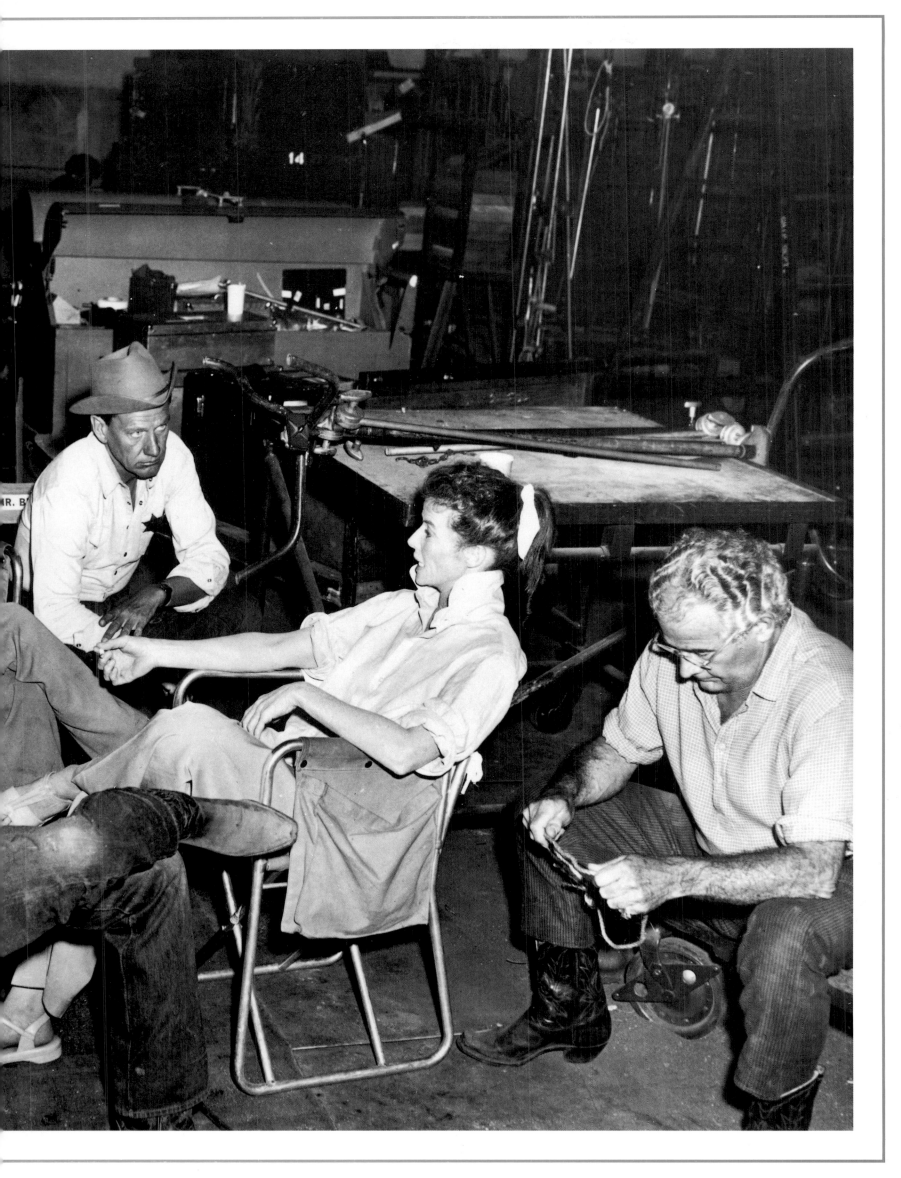

Above: Hepburn and Bob Hope made an unlikely couple in **The Iron Petticoat** (1956), a loose remake of Greta Garbo's **Ninotchka** (1939). Hepburn played a Soviet pilot who, seduced by lingerie and champagne, forsakes communism for capitalism. The film was not well received. Hepburn's and Hope's comedic skills were of a different ilk; she was from the school of light, sophisticated comedy, while Hope favored a broader humor. Ralph Thomas, the director, was too inexperienced to handle such diverse talents.

Above: Having waged the battle of the sexes in the court-room, in the political arena and on the golf course, Hepburn and Tracy moved the battle to the television newsroom in **The Desk Set** (1957). Based on the 1955 Broadway play, **The Desk Set** is the story of an electronics genius (Spencer Tracy) who invents a machine—an electric brain—which Bunny Watson, a reference librarian (Hepburn) fears will replace her.

Though **The Desk Set** is generally regarded as a second-rate film, Hepburn and Tracy were well-received and cred-ited with saving a weak script. This was the first time that they appeared in a color film together. In Britain, the film was released as **His Other Woman**.

Above: Hepburn as Mrs Venable in **Suddenly, Last Summer** (1959), Tennessee Williams' grim tale of homosexuality and cannibalism. Hepburn's performance as a woman who goes to extremes to hide her son's homosexuality was superb, but she absolutely hated the character and regretted making the film.

In addition to Kate's distaste for the story, production was acrimonious. Montgomery Clift's drug addiction made him unreliable, Elizabeth Taylor was upset at the gossip surrounding her marriage to Eddie Fisher, and Hepburn was dismayed when she discovered that she was being filmed in unflattering light. When filming was completed, she spit at producer Sam Speigel and director Joseph Mankiewicz.

Above: Elizabeth Taylor played the niece whom Mrs Venable wants to have lobotomized so that the details of her son's death will remain a secret. Montgomery Clift played the doctor who unravels the mystery by giving the niece a truth serum instead. Hepburn and Taylor were both nominated for an Academy Award, but essentially canceled each other out, with the Oscar going instead to Simone Signoret for **Room at the Top**.

Suddenly Last Summer was quite a departure from Hepburn's typical roles in light-hearted family entertainment and marked a change in Hollywood's approach to dealing with previously taboo topics. While most critics felt that the film helped pave the way for realism in films, others regarded it as sensationalism that pandered to the public's fear and ignorance of homosexuality. Williams himself was unhappy with the film version of his play.

Above: At an age when most actresses' careers are over, Hepburn entered an era of greatness with her performance as morphine-addicted Mary Tyrone in Eugene O'Neill's **Long Day's Journey Into Night** (1962). Hepburn agreed to do the film when she learned that not a word of O'Neill's play would be altered. Enthusiastic about the opportunity to finally do O'Neill, she was willing to take a tremendous salary cut, agreeing to only $25,000 instead of her usual $250,000.

The role was emotionally draining for Kate, leaving her exhausted at the end of the day. Director Sidney Lumet was amazed by her performance, observing 'It was the culmination of a lifetime of self-exploration; she found depths of feeling in herself that surprised and even shocked her.'

Facing page: A 1962 portrait of Hepburn, her beauty undimmed by time.

Above: Dubbed a 'social comedy,' **Guess Who's Coming to Dinner** (1967) revolves around Matt and Christina Drayton's (Spencer Tracy and Katharine Hepburn) reaction to their daughter's announcement that she is going to marry a black man. Lifelong liberals, they find their beliefs tested as they come to terms with the situation. Hepburn's niece, Katharine Houghton, played the daughter, while Sidney Poitier played her fiance. Despite the issues raised, the film skirts any serious treatment of the topic and was praised not as a social commentary, but rather for the sentimental occasion of the last screen effort by one of Hollywood's most famous and beloved duos.

Above: **Guess Who's Coming to Dinner** (1967) was the ninth and final Hepburn and Tracy film. In failing health, Tracy had not worked for a number of years, nor had Hepburn, so that she could be by his side. She saw the film as a perfect farewell vehicle for him, and indeed he died two weeks after the film was completed. Both stars garnered nominations for Academy Awards (Tracy's ninth nomination, Hepburn's tenth). Though Tracy lost to Rod Steiger for **In the Heat of the Night**, Hepburn was awarded her second Academy Award for Best Actress. William Rose also won for Best Original Screenplay.

All told, the film received 10 nominations for Academy Awards: Best Picture, Best Actor (Spencer Tracy), Best Actress (Hepburn), Best Director (Stanley Kramer), (Best Supporting Actor (Cecil Kellaway), and Best Supporting Actress (Beah Richards), as well as Editing, Art Direction, Music and Screenplay.

After Tracy's death, many assumed that Hepburn would again withdraw from the public eye. Instead she agreed to star with Peter O'Toole in **The Lion in Winter** (1968), an epic about Henry II of England and his banished wife, Eleanor of Aquitaine. Both stars were critically acclaimed, with John Russell Taylor of *The London Times* declaring Eleanor 'the performance of [Hepburn's] career.'

Above: Hepburn's performance as Eleanor of Aquitaine in
The Lion in Winter (1968) earned her back-to-back Oscars
in a tie vote with Barbra Streisand.

Above: Hepburn as Aurelia, the eccentric Parisian of **The Madwoman of Chaillot** (1969). This classic fantasy by Jean Giraudoux was to have been directed by John Huston, but he resigned over a disagreement about the script. His judgment served him well, for the film received poor reviews.

Above: In 1971, Hepburn tried her hand at Greek drama in Michael Cacoyannis' film adaptation of Euripides' *The Trojan Women* 'because my time is running out, and one wants to have tried everything.' In addition to Hepburn as Hecuba, the film featured a strong cast—Vanessa Redgrave, Genevieve Bujold and Irene Papas—but generally received poor reviews. Nevertheless, Hepburn's determination and unwavering sense of adventure cannot be faulted. As soon as filming was completed, she went on tour with *Coco*, a musical about the life of designer Coco Chanel.

Facing page: A publicity still from **The Madwoman of Chaillot** (1969).

Above: **Rooster Cogburn** (1975) gave audiences the chance to see two of Hollywood's favorite stars. John Wayne recreated his Academy Award-winning performance as the 'fat, one-eyed marshal' from **True Grit** and Hepburn played Eula Goodnight, a spinster out to avenge her father's death. Despite recent hip surgery, Hepburn insisted on doing all her own horseback riding and stunts, declaring 'I haven't waited all these years to do a cowboy picture with Wayne to give up a single moment of it now.'

Facing page, above: In 1976, Hepburn returned to Broadway in *A Matter of Gravity*, a story of an eccentric woman, Mrs Basil, who rejects modern life, locking herself away in her mansion. Her grandson attempts to change her point of view by introducing her to an assorted cast of free-thinking individuals. Critics and the public alike thoroughly enjoyed *A Matter of Gravity*, which was written by 87-year-old Enid Bagnold, the author of *National Velvet*.

Facing page, below: Hepburn appeared with Laurence Olivier in **Love Among the Ruins** (1975), a television movie directed by George Cukor.

Above: In uncharacteristic fashion, Hepburn joined Morley Safer for an interview on *60 Minutes*. Throughout her career, Hepburn did not disguise her disdain for the press. It was no secret that she hated to give interviews and would go to great lengths to avoid the press, regarding their questions as intrusions. She had even written an article for the *Virginia Law Review* on the individual's right to privacy.

After Tracy's death Hepburn was more open to talking with the press, and in 1978 she agreed to the *60 Minutes* appearance to help publicize the television movie, **The Corn Is Green** (1978), her final film with her old friend George Cukor.

Above and below: Scenes from **The Corn Is Green** (1978), the tale of Miss Moffatt, a schoolteacher in Wales who helps a young miner attain his goal of going to Oxford. At first, Hepburn had refused Cukor's request to appear in the movie, but when she read the script, she changed her mind: 'Oh indeed, a wonderful part. My, I laughed and I cried and cried. Lovely for me. Such a relief. A woman alive. Not half dead.'

Cukor was delighted to work with Kate again, declaring 'She surprises me in every scene. She has such freshness and spontaneity. She never goes for the obvious effect... she plays it with more understanding than she would have thirty years ago, more forthrightly and humorously.'

Above: Hepburn stands before a portrait of Spencer Tracy, her colleague and companion for close to 30 years. Theirs was a very private relationship that everyone knew about but no one talked about because that was the way Spence and Kate wanted it.

At first Hollywood was surprised by the relationship, for they were opposites. Hepburn considered herself fancy, like a dessert, while Tracy was basic, like a potato. He was a hard drinker; she rarely drank. He stayed away from politics (though he was a staunch supporter of Roosevelt); she was known for her outspoken, liberal beliefs. They came from diverse family backgrounds. His father had been a truck salesman; hers a noted surgeon. Tracy had worked a number of odd jobs to survive; Kate had never worried about money. Their acting styles were on opposite ends of the spectrum. Tracy was simple and direct in his approach. He was recognized as the consummate actor. Hepburn, on the other hand, had been criticized throughout her career for overplaying her lines, for being too mannered. Working with Tracy toned down her style. In short, they seemed an unlikely couple, but their relationship endured until his death in 1967.

These pages: **On Golden Pond** (1981) featured Katharine Hepburn and Henry Fonda as Ethel and Norman Thayer, with Jane Fonda as their estranged daughter. The plot focused on the relationship of the husband and wife as they come to terms with aging and with their troubled relationship with their daughter. A sentimental heart-warmer, **On Golden Pond** owes part of its success to the audience knowing that they were watching more than a movie about a crusty old guy making peace with his daughter—they were watching a dying Henry Fonda resolve similar problems with his own daughter. Henry Fonda lived long enough to witness the film's success and finally be recognized with a long-deserved Academy Award. Hepburn won her fourth Academy Award, making her the all-time Oscar champ.

These pages: Hepburn in **The Ultimate Solution of Grace Quigley** (1984), a black comedy about an old woman who hires an assassin to do her in. Instead, the two of them join forces, ending the lives of other old people who are unhappy and ready to die. Hepburn had been interested in doing this film for 10 years, but the studios were reluctant to deal with the topic. Anthony Harvey, who had worked with Hepburn on **The Lion in Winter** (1968), directed the film.

Upon meeting her costar, Nick Nolte (*above*), who had a reputation for drinking and partying, Hepburn immediately made it her mission to put him back on the straight and narrow, as she had tried with many of her costars over the years. Nolte was able to overlook Kate's zealousness, and observed, 'She's a legend, but once you get beyond that she's just a cranky old broad who can sometimes be a whole lot of fun.'

In 1992, Katharine Hepburn appeared in what is expected to be her final film, **The Man Upstairs**. A made-for-television film co-starring Ryan O'Neal, it first aired on CBS on 6 December 1992.

Since Kate has been plagued by health problems the last few years, the cast and crew were worried about her doing a scene that called for her to run up a flight of stairs. In true Hepburn fashion, she took the stairs two at a time.

Filmography

Cinema

A Bill of Divorcement (1932)
Christopher Strong (1933)
Morning Glory (1933)
Little Women (1933)
Spitfire (1934)
The Little Minister (1934)
Break of Hearts (1935)
Alice Adams (1935)
Sylvia Scarlett (1936)
Mary of Scotland (1936)
A Woman Rebels (1936)
Quality Street (1937)
Stage Door (1937)
Bringing Up Baby (1938)
Holiday (1938)
The Philadelphia Story (1940)
Woman of the Year (1942)
Keeper of the Flame (1942)
Stage Door Canteen (1943)
Dragon Seed (1944)
Without Love (1945)
Undercurrent (1946)
Sea of Grass (1947)
Song of Love (1947)
State of the Union (1948)
Adam's Rib (1949)
The African Queen (1951)
Pat and Mike (1952)
Summertime (1955)
The Rainmaker (1956)
The Iron Petticoat (1956)
The Desk Set (1957)
Suddenly Last Summer (1959)
Long Day's Journey into Night (1962)
Guess Who's Coming to Dinner (1967)
The Lion in Winter (1968)
The Madwoman of Chaillot (1969)
The Trojan Women (1972)
Rooster Cogburn (1975)
Olly Olly Oxen Free (1981)
On Golden Pond (1981)
The Ultimate Solution of Grace Quigley (1984)

Stage

The Czarina (bit part; 1928)
The Cradle Snatchers (bit part; 1928)
The Big Pond (1928)
These Days (1928)
Holiday (understudy; 1928)
Death Takes a Holiday (1929)
A Month in the Country (1930)
A Romantic Young Lady (summer stock; 1930)
The Admiral Crichton (summer stock; 1930)
Just Married (summer stock; 1931)
The Cat and the Canary (summer stock; 1931)
The Man Who Came Back (summer stock; 1931)
The Animal Kingdom (1931)
The Warrior's Husband (1931)
The Bride the Sun Shines On (summer stock; 1932)
The Lake (1933)
Jane Eyre (1936)
The Philadelphia Story (1939)
Without Love (1942)
As You Like It (1950)
The Millionairess (1952)
The Merchant of Venice (summer tour; 1955)
The Taming of the Shrew (summer tour; 1955)
Measure for Measure (summer tour; 1955)
The Merchant of Venice (1957)
Much Ado About Nothing (1957)
Twelfth Night (1960)
Antony and Cleopatra (1960)
Coco (1969)
A Matter of Gravity (1976)
The West Side Waltz (1981)

Television

A Delicate Balance (1972)
The Glass Menagerie (1973)
Love Among the Ruins (1975)
The Corn Is Green (1978)
Mrs Delafield Wants to Marry (1986)
Laura Lansing Slept Here (1988)
The Man Upstairs (1992)

Index

Overleaf: A portrait of Kate from the early 1940s. This was an important time in her life. She had successfully engineered her stage and screen comeback with **The Philadelphia Story** (1940). It was also during this era that she met and fell in love with Spencer Tracy.

111